Insect World

Fireflies

by Mari Schuh

Bullfrog
Books

Ideas for Parents and Teachers

Bullfrog Books let children practice reading informational text at the earliest reading levels. Repetition, familiar words, and photo labels support early readers.

Before Reading

• Discuss the cover photo. What does it tell them?

• Look at the picture glossary together. Read and discuss the words.

Read the Book

• "Walk" through the book and look at the photos. Let the child ask questions. Point out the photo labels.

• Read the book to the child, or have him or her read independently.

After Reading

• Prompt the child to think more. Ask: Have you ever seen a firefly light up at night? Where was it flying?

Dedicated to Mike and Amanda Fox—MS

Bullfrog Books are published by Jump!
5357 Penn Avenue South
Minneapolis, MN 55419
www.jumplibrary.com

Library of Congress Cataloging-in-Publication Data

Schuh, Mari C., 1975- author.
  Fireflies / by Mari Schuh.
    pages cm. -- (Insect world)
  Audience: 5-8.
  Audience: K to grade 3.
  Summary: "This photo-illustrated book for early readers tells why fireflies flash their lights and briefly describes their life cycle. Includes picture glossary."-- Provided by publisher.
  Includes bibliographical references and index.
  ISBN 978-1-62031-084-7 (hardcover) --
ISBN 978-1-62496-152-6 (ebook)
  1. Fireflies--Juvenile literature. I. Title.
II. Series: Schuh, Mari C., 1975- Insect world.
  QL596.L28S38 2015
  595.76'44--dc23

                          2013037889

Series Editor: Rebecca Glaser
Series Designer: Ellen Huber
Book Designer: Anna Peterson
Photo Researcher: Kurtis Kinneman

Photo Credits: Alex Wild, 5, 10–11, 14–15, 23br; Atsuo Fujimaru/Minden Pictures, 12–13, 23bl; Dale Darwin/Getty Images, 7; Imagemore/SuperStock, 1, 6, 22; Jeun-ven Shih | Dreamstime.com, cover, 23tl; John Tyler, 18 inset; Norbert Wu/Science Faction/Corbis, 24; Picture Press/Alamy, 18–19, 23tr; Pigdevil Photo/Shutterstock, 16; Satoshi Kuribayashi/Minden Pictures, 17; Suede Chen/Shutterstock, 3, 4, 8–9; TommyIX/iStock, 22; Westend61/SuperStock, 20–21

Printed in the United States of America at Corporate Graphics, in North Mankato, Minnesota.
6-2014
10 9 8 7 6 5 4 3 2 1

Table of Contents

Bright Bugs 4

Parts of a Firefly 22

Picture Glossary 23

Index 24

To Learn More 24

Bright Bugs

It is summer. It is a dark night.

What is flashing?
A lot of fireflies!

A firefly is a beetle.

Look at its body.

It glows.

The firefly wants to mate.

He flies into the sky.

He flashes his light.

Blink. Blink.

Who will see him?

A female firefly sits
on a leaf.

She sees him.

She flashes her light.

Blink. Blink.

The firefly finds her.

They mate.

Later, she lays 500 eggs.
She puts them on wet soil.

They glow.

The eggs grow.
The larvas hatch
in four weeks.

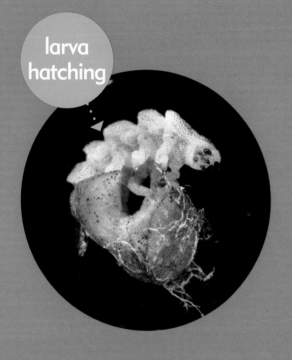

larva
hatching

larva

Soon, they will grow wings.

They will light up the night.

Blink! Blink!

Parts of a Firefly

hard wings
Two strong wings that protect a firefly's soft wings.

antenna
A feeler on a firefly's head that it uses to smell and feel.

soft wings
Two wings a firefly uses to fly.

leg
A firefly has six legs, like all insects.

Picture Glossary

beetle
An insect with two hard wings and two soft wings.

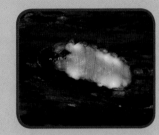

larva
A young firefly that hatches from an egg; it does not have wings.

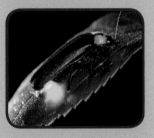

female
An animal that can lay eggs or give birth to young.

mate
To join together to make young.

Index

beetles 6

eggs 16, 18

female 13

flashing 5, 10, 13

flying 10

glowing 7, 17

hatching 18

larva 18

mating 8, 14

night 4, 20

wings 20

To Learn More

Learning more is as easy as 1, 2, 3.

1) Go to www.factsurfer.com

2) Enter "fireflies" into the search box.

3) Click the "Surf" button to see a list of websites.

With factsurfer.com, finding more information is just a click away.